I0624257

REALITY HUNGER
ON KARL OVE KNAUSGAARD'S MY STRUGGLE

ARROWSMITH

PRESS

Reality Hunger: On Karl Ove Knausgaard's *My Struggle*
by William Pierce
© 2016 William Pierce

First Edition, Second Printing
ISBN: 979-8-9904050-3-5

Designed by Erica Mena.

Boston—New York—San Francisco—Baghdad
San Juan—Kyiv—Istanbul—Santiago, Chile
Beijing—Paris—London—Cairo—Madrid
Milan—Melbourne—Jerusalem—Darfur

11 Chestnut St.
Medford, MA 02155
arrowsmithpress@gmail.com

www.arrowsmithpress.org

REALITY HUNGER
ON KARL OVE KNAUSGAARD'S
MY STRUGGLE

BY WILLIAM PIERCE

PART I: THE PLEASURES OF BEING ALIVE

> It was like / A new knowledge of reality.
> —Wallace Stevens,
> "Not Ideas About the Thing but the Thing Itself"

Just days after finishing Book One of *My Struggle*, an unusual six-part novel, I took a train from Boston to New York to see if I could meet the author, Karl Ove Knausgaard. This was in June 2014, after the release of Book Three. His New York Public Library appearance was sold out, but there were two other events scheduled, and the writers lined up to hold public conversations with him gave a hint of the excitement people were feeling: Zadie Smith, Nicole Krauss, Jeffrey Eugenides. In my duffel I'd packed Book Two, but already the first volume was enough to make the trip a kind of pilgrimage for me.

My Struggle—3,600 pages in Norwegian, which Don Bartlett is translating at a rate of one book per year—sets out in astonishing and dispassionately forthright detail the struggles both large and incidental of a life: a boy, a young man, a father, navigating his days in Norway and Sweden. Knausgaard has a gift for analyzing precisely the self at the center of the narrative without in the least neglecting the pleasures of being alive. Rarely have I felt more gripped by a novel.

I arrived at Community Bookstore in Park Slope two and a

half hours early, having mistaken the start time. Already there were people waiting. I left and came back. By then, with an hour to go, only a few seats were available. Two women stood up so I could climb past their chairs to an out-of-the-way bench that no one had noticed. People were comparing how far they'd read, talking about the rave reviews, commenting on his good looks. In *The New York Times* ArtsBeat blog the next day, John Williams wrote: "About 30 minutes before the start [...] people packed the entire space in a scene more reminiscent of the calm before an indie-rock storm than an author appearance. Ezra Goldstein, an owner of the store, approached a microphone. 'Don't get excited,' he said. 'This is just a sound check.'"

My imagination had constructed two not entirely unrelated images of who the writer might be: the taciturn, somewhat antisocial Karl Ove, the character from the novel (its protagonist shares Knausgaard's name and biographical details), or, alternately, the dismissive hero suggested by the author photographs and some of the early reviews—an overnight sensation only accidentally literary, whose cigarettes, long hair, and sex appeal seemed to emphasize offhandedness. The first of these would be impossible to get to know, the second would be insufferable.

When he arrived, we applauded and caught images on our phones. He was more handsome and magnetic than in pictures, his silvery hair combed straight back, his public smile infectious. But during the ensuing conversation with Nicole Krauss, I was struck by how private the hour felt, how much Knausgaard seemed to think things through as he spoke rather than reciting paragraphs he'd delivered a hundred times before. He talked slowly, with his shoulders hunched, his hands now clasped, now gesturing, his forehead wrinkled. He came across as modest, thoughtful—full of hurt and humor. Or maybe it was jetlag. I was as drawn to the man as I'd been to Book One.

The next night I waited for him again, at McNally Jackson Books in Greenwich Village. A line extended halfway down the block—100 people or more—even after the lower level, where he'd be appearing with Zadie Smith, had filled. Some in the audience stood behind bookshelves, others sat on the wide steps, and still more listened from upstairs. It reminded me of accounts of Dostoevsky's reception late in his life, when an adoring public thronged his dedication of the Pushkin Monument.

When the Q&A at Community Bookstore ended, the entire audience—maybe 200 people in a space designed for far fewer—transformed into a signing line. I hung back, watching and listening, hoping my friendship with his American publisher would give me license to meet Knausgaard at a quieter moment and join in for whatever was happening after. And that's how it went. We sat in folding chairs on the back patio—me, the editors of Archipelago Books, the staff and owners of the bookstore, a representative from his Norwegian publishing house, and Knausgaard, drinking can after can of Dale's Pale Ale, a few of us bumming Knausgaard's Marlboros—and talked late into the night.

Δ

I didn't plan to write about it. I simply wanted to thank whoever had written those pages. But on the train ride home, when I turned to my iPad and the many reviews and responses I hadn't read yet, the first I landed on was William Deresiewicz's in *The Nation*. He writes of *My Struggle*, which was originally published in Norwegian from 2009 to 2011:

> The book [...] is not exactly a minute-by-minute account of the author's life, with all the tedium that that implies, but it comes as close as you could wish [...]. Volume I devotes some sixty pages to a New Year's Eve the year the author turns 16: putzing around at home until it's time to get going, smuggling beer with a friend, hitching to a lousy party, getting the brush-off from a popular girl.

Nothing "happens *in the writing*," he tells us. And he quotes James Wood and Zadie Smith, big fans of Knausgaard, on such things as the transparency of the prose and the writer's "apparent refusal [...] to shape or select"—or, as Deresiewicz translates this, his "renunciation of art."

For me this was akin to being told the emperor had no clothes when I could plainly see what he was wearing. During those New Year's Eve scenes, I'd felt a particular tension to find out what happens next through all of the beer-smuggling and the ride-hitching. And what's more, I felt Knausgaard giving and withholding information in a way calculated to lure me.

Even positive reviewers struggle to say how Knausgaard keeps us interested, as Hari Kunzru suggests in *The Guardian*:

> The commentary on *My Struggle* tends to focus, as I have in these paragraphs, on the phenomenon of the book's publication, rather than the writing itself. It is peculiarly difficult to get a grip on what makes the book so compelling, because much of it appears painfully banal.

The slyness of his word *appears* is wonderful. *To the Lighthouse* can appear banal, too, if you strip it down to what happens.

But many reviewers seem to have taken to heart Knausgaard's formulation, which he repeats frequently, about putting everything into this one project, writing it all, as if *My Struggle* were a brain dump. If we decide the author has artlessly regurgitated what he remembers and by dumb luck the vast spill of it just magically works (or not), we can skip asking how the book functions. We can stop looking for what it's about. We can believe, as Deresiewicz seems to, that it renounces meaning. And we can start making Knausgaard whatever we need him to be, or whatever the novel and our collective moment seem to imply he is.

When I was 12 and 13, I was in frequent fistfights at school. I hardly bothered to dream of being included in the social goings-on in town, not wanting to be picked on and get myself into more fights. So, using the excuse of distance—we lived miles outside the then-small town of Hershey, Pennsylvania—I spent weekends in the basement, organizing my collections of army gear, animal skeletons, rocks, beer cans, and HO trains, or reading Hardy Boys and then sci-fi and fantasy novels.

Maybe that goes some way toward explaining why I care instantly when Karl Ove wants to join a New Year's party he's not invited to. The plan is, he'll go to a party where only his friend Jan Vidar knows anyone, and then, at midnight, when Norwegians take to the streets to celebrate, he'll switch—if he dares—to spend time with his classmates. As he and Jan Vidar arrange to get beer, as he kills time at home, as he walks in the dark to Jan Vidar's house, as they bus into town together, I want him to succeed. I also feel his anxiety, which in the narrative is expressed only in the drawn-out complexity of his preparations. The preparations bear his anxiety, and our attention bears ours, whether present or remembered.

For each of us, *My Struggle* seems to be a different book. Maybe Kunzru means that the surprise of *My Struggle* is not just how compelling it is, but how difficult it is to describe that compulsion in a way that seems to apply or transfer to other readers. Let enthusiasm beget enthusiasm—but each person's addiction to *My Struggle* feels personal.

Δ

Knausgaard has said he was experimenting with how far he could take digression, but the novelty here is that one reader's digression can be another's main thread. For me, the risk of boredom came only late in the book, as Karl Ove cleans his grandmother's house after his father's death. The details are exquisite, but the whole affair goes on disproportionately long. As James Wood points out in *The New Yorker*, this thoroughness immerses us in Karl Ove's emotional transference, the enacting of his grief and embarrassment. While we can hardly mistake the suspense in a Tom Clancy novel—where it begins and what causes it—Knausgaard's dramas are, like the work of another hero of mine, the Swiss novelist Robert Walser, of such consistently small amplitude that every footfall can either fade away or resound like an earthquake.

Book One opens not with narrative but with an extended consideration of how Westerners spirit away the dead. "What exactly it is that is being repressed, however, is not so easy to say. It cannot be death itself, for its presence in society is much too prominent." A sensibility asserts itself immediately—curious, skeptical, matter-of-fact, dissatisfied with things-as-they-are, intent on finding less obvious meanings, but, especially, committed to giving voice to what others keep to themselves. "The way we remove bodies has never been the subject of debate, it has always been just something we have done […]: if your father dies on the lawn one windswept Sunday in autumn, you carry him indoors if you can, and if you can't, you at least cover him with a blanket." This is a "collective act of repression."

Soon enough, on page 11, a scene opens, and we are watching the child Karl Ove sitting alone watching TV. What he sees on TV surprises him. He goes off to tell someone, but the only person home is his father, a man he's afraid of. With this, a trademark oscillation is established, from reflective essay to in-the-moment narrative and back again. The earliest scenes are set in the Norwegian town of Kristiansand, where the young Karl Ove lives with his parents and brother. Then—in another of the book's oscillations—the story jumps forward in time, to the Swedish city of Malmö and the "present" of Karl Ove's adulthood: "As I sit here writing this, I recognize that more than thirty years have passed." Now Karl Ove is the father of three children. He is married and a writer. In the shift from essay to narrative, Knausgaard asserts the freedom to move thematically and associatively. In the shift from childhood to adulthood, he frees the book from expectations of chronology and builds in a reflective layer—the perspective of intervening years. Malmö represents the book's temporal limit (*My Struggle* moves backward and forward, but rarely all the way to "now") and gives the first signal that we might be reading memoir. Karl Ove—the boy who cries too much and has a stutter—declares that he's the author.

Finishing those early sections, I felt I would follow the story anywhere, so addictive was the odd but familiar sensibility that gives the book its atmosphere. I craved the immediacy of it, the unrushed urgency, wanted access to that rebellious openness. The Malmö sections gripped me more personally: here was Karl Ove chafing against domestic life just as I was, questioning the decision to become a parent just as I did, loving his kids as I love mine. Simple identification maybe, but tuned to a particular range of the bandwidth. Whenever the narrative returned to Kristiansand, everything was pleasant anticipation for me, a digression that, page by page, amped up the sense that something big was coming. I read on.

The long arc of that suspense didn't stop me from feeling other, shorter-lived tensions along the way, like those leading up to the New Year's party, and I'm convinced this nesting of one set of expectations within another is not something I'm alone in experiencing with Knausgaard. The split-screen view—our mind's eye looking ahead while also held by the present—reminds me of another celebrated storyteller, Queen Scheherazade in *One Thousand and One Nights*. Her stories are freighted beyond what happens in them—each is a lifeboat keeping her alive, but only as long as the story is absorbing enough to make us and Shahryar forget she has an ulterior motive.

With a novel that operates like the unstressed Japanese language, in which every syllable is given equal weight, Knausgaard achieves texture in part by empowering the reader's imagination to impose its own emphasis. Again and again, I am like the reader of John Cheever's "Montraldo." Its narrator steals a diamond ring from Tiffany's in the first paragraph—a setup so powerful that we stay alert and anxious through a quiet story in which thieving and its consequences never come up again. But in *My Struggle*, what suspends me, what keeps me engaged, may or may not be the same thing that propels another reader. In her *Slate* essay "Her Struggle," Katie Roiphe reads Knausgaard for the novel's takes on domesticity and child-rearing; my friend Rosamond craves the passages on cooking and food; another friend, Sumita, listens for Karl Ove's outsized sense of responsibility, recognizing her own. Different readers are ignited by different reappearances and resolutions. As Francine Prose wrote in *Harper's*: "It is Knausgaard's structure as much as his subject that shades every moment, no matter how seemingly mundane, with significance."

Knausgaard says he wrote *My Struggle* quickly. He says he was letting it all out and that he refrained from writing only what his body wouldn't *let* him write. Of course, when a scene or image came to mind, he couldn't necessarily write it straight away without interfering with the tale he was in the middle of. But I'd go further and say he made a fetish of holding in as much as letting out. His restraint shapes every page of the book. He alludes to this in an interview with Kyle Buckley at *Hazlitt*: "There's one thing that I'm interested in in the whole book, or a couple of things, and everything else is excluded. [...] So it's very narrow, even if it's 3,500 pages, it's very narrow." His urge to write each sequence to its conclusion—and yet, often, not to do it all at once but to braid in other narratives—is a structuring urge. The smallest moments are tributaries that lead to the larger streams and into the main current. Everything helps him tell what he's telling, do what he's doing—it all gives rise to, and supports, a larger point. Knausgaard is a composer who takes opportunities when they come, bringing back the French horn to recall an earlier passage, letting the piccolo reprise the theme first played long before by the oboe.

Everywhere, Knausgaard cultivates a parallel-worlds sense of what is through-line and what is digression—while I read for a parent's chafing against domestic life, you read for ambivalence about a father. He suspends us but doesn't micromanage what is the exhale and what the held breath. This is mastery analogous to the kind Julio Cortázar achieved when, with *Hopscotch* (1963), he gave us a book whose chapters could be read in different orders. Did he write the book you read if you encounter *Hopscotch* in an order that's never been tried? Of course he did. Yet the possibilities are beyond counting.

Δ

In its parts, and in the whole they form, this massive canvas has a meaning beyond its themes of childhood and child-rearing, losing a parent and falling in love. With *My Struggle*, Knausgaard makes a bid—a huge, quixotic one—to restore the possibility of awe, which rises less from the length of the book or its focus on his life than from its colossal ambitions for what a novel can achieve.

In Book One, the narrator pauses to describe a shift in the history of Western art. Norwegian painter Edvard Munch represents the new mode:

Whereas man was subordinate to the Divine through to the Age of Enlightenment, and to the landscape he was depicted in during Romanticism—the mountains are vast and intense, the sea is vast and intense, even the trees are vast and intense while humans, without exception, are small—the situation is reversed with Munch. [...] The mountains, the sea, the trees, and the forests, everything is colored by humanness. Not human actions and external life, but human feelings and inner life.

In Munch, the human infuses everything in the frame; every tree has become an expression of emotion. There's a terrible loss in this: "Here we are in a world of images where the expression itself is everything, which of course means that there is no longer any dynamism between the outer and the inner. [...] Everything has become intellect, even our bodies, they aren't bodies anymore, but ideas of bodies."

From the first pages of Book One, Knausgaard intends a corrective. He wants to tease aside emotion and leave only the ungraspable strangeness of what remains when we die, the radical otherness of material things. "Death," as the narrator expresses it later, "is the last great beyond."

Knausgaard brings back landscape and scale, he restores object and sequence. He attempts (and fails, sure) to re-achieve the sublime, to situate us in our true context of accident, coincidence, surprise, and mystery.

Yet while making the human small in the landscape, he also keeps the human where we know it has to be in our lives: at the center. He is resolutely if regretfully post-Freud, post-Derrida. Every life is experienced from the vantage of a single consciousness, we're all bounded by ourselves, held to the limits of our own perception. We can't escape even the awareness of those limitations anymore. In this light, Deresiewicz's charge that implication—and to a large extent this means emotion—figures less in *My Struggle* than in nearly every other novel becomes the description of a hard-won technique. Implications appear in the background, while objects and landscapes are situated in the foreground. In fact, they haven't dominated this much since perhaps the novels of Thomas Hardy. Kitchens appear as kitchens, skies as skies, coffeepots as coffeepots. They do not figure as metaphors, they don't mirror events or amplify our sense of a human drama. They don't function as a carefully timed soundtrack. There isn't a sudden thaw when someone's happy, as in Flaubert's *Madame Bovary*, icicles dripping in the sunshine. A cold day is just butt-cold, no matter how much pleasure or relief enters the frame. This attachment to the material, to everyday objects, shrinks the human even while the structure of the novel affirms at every moment that we're helpless to witness anything except through the lens of our witnessing. Knausgaard paints a Constable using the palette of Munch.

Δ

At times it might seem that Knausgaard isn't fashioning much of anything. His style, or seeming lack of it, has been a subject of discussion—but what is it that constitutes style? I remember Michael Hofmann saying he's no fan of Kafka because Kafka is not a stylist. I'm a fan of Kafka in part because he *is*. Dostoevsky certainly isn't. There maybe everyone can agree. Russians tend not to give a damn about him anymore because, they insist, he was such a terrible prose writer. I love Hofmann's translation of *The Radetzky March* by Joseph Roth. Roth is a stylist in the way of Saul Bellow or Thomas Mann—consistently exploring language while also bounded by a traditionalist's sense of what goes into a literary style. That kind of writing can feel age-old even when it's new. Virginia Woolf, in her fiction at least, resists such classicism. Her turns feel radically unexpected, from the sentence level to the whole. But where does the difference lie? Does her truest revolution take place in diction, syntax, rhetoric, figure, structure, or in all of the above?

Despite the lack of ornament, Knausgaard's prose has a distinctive flavor. There are subtle shifts from book to book, yet the matter-of-factness, his drive to lay things out without ego or deference, gives the prose the same appealing flatness you hear in his speaking voice. Even as its timbre rises and falls, a deep monotone rides beneath, as in the background of Gregorian chant. There are exceptions—moments of goofiness, a memory of enthusiasm that colors the prose—but the baseline is the note of life forthrightly and unceremoniously considered, as if Knausgaard were looking back on the world after death, with a great fond tolerance, a highly interested disinterest.

Deresiewicz is underwhelmed by the plainness of Knausgaard's seeing. He quotes what he takes to be a no-brainer of a comparison between two descriptions—one that works for him and one that doesn't:

> I happen to be reading Updike at the moment. Here is his description of a young woman in an unfamiliar surrounding: "She is serious, a serious small-faced animal sniffing out her new lair." We don't just see her; we see into her. Here is Knausgaard's description of a girl he liked at age 11, his first serious crush, as emotion-saturated an experience as one can imagine: "She wasn't very tall and she was wearing a pink jacket, a light-blue skirt, and thin, white stockings. Her nose was small, her mouth large, and she had a little cleft in her chin." And that's the first time that he catches sight of her, no less. I'm almost ready to fall in love myself.

For him the winner in this stylistic comparison is clear enough for mockery. And it's true—there's nothing in Knausgaard's words here to mark them out as part of a literary masterpiece. But I don't see Updike's young woman at all. To me, in the description Deresiewicz quotes, she's buried in cleverness.

Again and again, a split opens between what *should* work and what does. In *Aspects of the Novel*, E. M. Forster shrugs at the then fairly new orthodoxy, championed by Henry James, that point of view should remain consistent throughout a novel. "The whole intricate question of method," Forster writes, "resolves itself not into formulae but into the power of the writer to bounce the reader into accepting what he says […]. Dickens bounces us, so that we do not mind the shiftings of the viewpoint." Knausgaard, by analogy, bounces us also, yet for some critics a question has remained about whether it's okay to let ourselves be bounced.

This recalls Kunzru's canny formulation that much of Knausgaard "appears painfully banal." In this, Knausgaard follows the audacious Flaubert, who starts his account of Yonville and the Bovarys by emphasizing how boring the town is. *Madame Bovary* mocks the falsely exotic—"pale landscapes of dithyrambic lands, that often show us at once palm-trees and firs"—and promises a deeper source of traction. If we don't want to soak in a book's atmosphere, then what's the book worth? And if we do, who needs melodrama in far-off climes? It's easy to forget how radically and consciously Flaubert was turning away from big plot, swashbuckling, political intrigue. We think of *Madame Bovary* as eventful. But the story is local, small-scale, domestic. While vowing to remove the author from the novel, to draw himself back to the point of absence, Flaubert saturated the book with a purified essence of himself, a sensibility that's his alone. This is the reason the "boring" material of Yonville—this nothing of a small town, these unimportant people, a small-time doctor and his unfaithful wife— grips us even when it's least eventful.

Flaubert's direction was a new one, and now extends to Knausgaard. He doesn't rely on literary floridries or carefully wrought surfaces, and he turns away from many of the common crutches, our palm trees—even from some that Flaubert not only retained but also helped to develop as if in recompense for what he was giving up. And in the process Knausgaard shows that when nothing occurs beyond the ordinary—things like death and breakfast—and language is demystified enough to make Wittgenstein proud, the resulting quiet can open up space for a different kind of attention.

Above all, Knausgaard has dispensed with *effusions* of literary style. There is tremendous style here, endless moves that take brio and technical skill, but Knausgaard, rejecting embellishment, doesn't let them declare themselves. On my trip to New York I met with novelist Sheila Kohler, who happened to be carrying Book One in her bag. A few days later she emailed me to marvel at its clever structuring: "The greatest of writers, of course, hoodwink us the best," she wrote, "making us feel they are simply relating life. But if you look carefully they never are."

PART II: THE ABSENCE TAKES A SHAPE

I remembered every detail of the day when [Swedish Prime Minister Olof Palme's] murder had been made public. What I had been doing, what I had been thinking. It had been a Saturday. Mom had been ill and I had caught the bus to town with Jan Vidar. We had been seventeen years old. If the Palme murder had not taken place, the day would have vanished, as all the others had. All the hours, all the minutes, all the conversations, all the thoughts, all the events. Into a pool of oblivion with everything else.

—Karl Ove, *My Struggle*, Book Two

Thinking about Knausgaard and form—his frustration with the ready-made configurations of the novel—reminded me of the Spanish philosopher José Ortega y Gasset writing on handshakes. In *Man and People* (1957), he goes on about handshakes with the same atomizing tenacity that Knausgaard brings to descriptions of making lunch:

I did not invent [the handshake] or think it on my own account, I copy or repeat it from others, from everybody else who does it, from "people." [...] I, a human being, find myself executing an act that lacks two of the indispensable characteristics of every strictly human action—originating intellectually in the subject who performs it and being engendered in his will. […] Very well—but who forces us? There is no doubt about the answer. It is usage. […] Usage [is] custom, and custom is a certain mode of behavior, a type of action which has become customary, that is, habitual.

I want to quote Ortega a little further, but taking the received or conventional forms of the novel to be the subject instead of Ortega's handshakes: "They were genuine human experiences which, so it seems, became survivals, human petrifactions" by dint of being repeated without reference to their original purpose or meaning. They were "not lived experience, but only its slough, residuum, corpse, skeleton, or fossil." What developed from the needs of individuals—writers, in the case of the novel—becomes formulaic, imposed where it doesn't naturally belong.

David Shields famously grew tired of the same old, same old and gave up on writing novels, opting instead to mash up other people's words and then complain that he had to give them credit. Knausgaard arrived at a similar dead end, as he told *Bookforum*: "It seemed to me that fiction was everywhere—TV-news, newspapers, films, and books all provide a flood of stories, a continuous dramatization of the world. So what I did, naively, was to try to take the world back. That's why I describe all these details in *My Struggle*." Unlike Shields, he neither gave up on nor inveighed against the novel, but took the braver step of dispensing with everything that felt ossified and restrictive to him. His advance was to trust that a writer versed in the techniques of narrative does well to subvert his self-editor—not as a writing exercise merely, or to free himself from block, but to reach yet deeper instincts for what to tell and how to tell it.

Here we have two different kinds of reality hunger. One is a hunger for reality as the word is used in "reality television." Shields named his manifesto *Reality Hunger*—but mash-ups are stagings, manipulations, falsest where they pretend to be real. The other is a hunger to probe and prod reality, to turn it up like fresh soil, to let it take a shape as close to organic as possible. It presses against the real in such an insistent way that we begin to sense the contours of an irreducible "distance between reality and the portrayal of reality," as Karl Ove has it, describing his favorite pre-Impressionist paintings:

> [I]t was doubtless in this interlying space where it "happened," where it appeared, whatever it was I saw, when the world seemed to step forward from the world. When you didn't just see the incomprehensible in it but came very close to it. Something that didn't speak, and that no words could grasp, consequently forever out of our reach, yet within it, for not only did it surround us, we were ourselves part of it, we were ourselves of it.

This is a challenge to memory and imagination. It seeks what can't be portrayed, the hyperpresence or thereness of every real moment, by coming so close to it that the absence takes a shape.

I loved hearing Knausgaard insist at Community Bookstore that his approach, too, would lose immediacy and come to feel as conventional as what it refused to imitate. Every gesture "dies as it's being born," as Ortega has it. Which is why—Knausgaard went on—art has to change from generation to generation: not out of any blind or merely experimental urge toward newness, but because we need, time and again, to break through the shell that forms and find something that elicits or holds or seems to reproduce the artist's truest self.

Δ

As I've mentioned, the protagonist of *My Struggle*, who speaks in first person, is "Karl Ove Knausgaard." Karl Ove hints in Book One that he's terrible at understanding other people. In his high school days, he tells us derisively,

> I actually regarded myself as a sound judge of character.
> I had a gift, or so I had deluded myself into thinking,
> it was something I was good at. Understanding others.
> While I myself was more of a mystery.
>
> How stupid can you get.

This is the tangled truth of what happens inside a head: how we overestimate ourselves, how we ridicule the beliefs we've outgrown. It may even—who knows?—express how Knausgaard the author (sometimes?) views himself. But that doesn't mean the narrator Karl Ove is speaking accurately about himself or the author.

What all of this implies is a matryoshka: the narrator Karl Ove's thoughts about his younger self might or might not be accurate about that younger self; might or might not apply to the adult Karl Ove; might or might not, if they apply, be accurate about him. They might resemble the author Knausgaard's thoughts now, or years ago, or thoughts he's only imagined thinking. When I consider how tangled the heart is, how often a feeling arrives with its opposite, I wonder how we could accept any expression of ourselves as a fair facsimile of who we are and what we think, even at a given moment. I take Karl Ove to be one of many specters of the author. I'd say the same thing about the characters in just about every book I love.

Δ

Simplicity and concreteness were not a given for Knausgaard, but a praxis. His writing can be dense, over-synapsed with implication. But not in the first three books, at least, of *My Struggle*. He chooses straightforwardness.

In Book Two, Karl Ove describes two "worlds"—one in which we live, where the seasons change and gnats land in our eyes, and one in which we think, a world filled with "secondary phenomena" and organized into "fields." Knausgaard reverses the usual relationship between the actual and the intellectual by subordinating the world of abstract ideas to the world of the domestic and everyday. The essays are not an attempt to analyze the life lived in these pages. They don't theorize truths that arise from the scenes. Instead, the scenes give us the sensibility, and the sensibility gives us the essays: the scenes dramatize the growth of the self that ends up thinking in those ways. There's a disconnect, then—of the left-brain, right-brain sort—between the ruminations in the book and the actions, but very little feeling of separation … maybe because we recognize the split from our own lives. Knausgaard found a means of letting us watch a life while also hearing the thoughts that the life gave rise to, without artificially binding the two.

The simplicity of the prose leaves the field open for a rare effect, when suddenly the language turns gorgeous. Just when its quiet has brought us to a new receptiveness, as if not only our skin but now the finest cilia are engaged, the volume rises. The spare sentences bloom, turn figurative. Color and valence shift, and we find ourselves moved by the smallest effects.

In the first paragraph below, the narrator considers the way his grandmother has just spoken to him:

> Something in her tone made me look at her. She had never spoken to me like that before. The strange thing was that it didn't change her as much as it changed me. That was how she must have spoken to Dad of late. She had addressed him not me. And that was not how she would have addressed Dad if Grandad had been alive.

That was the tone between mother and son when no one else was there.

   I didn't think that she had mistaken me for Dad, only that she was talking out of habit, like a ship continuing to glide through the water after the engines had been switched off. [...]

   Grandma whistled and drummed her fingers on the table. She had done that for as long as I could remember. There was something good about seeing it, for so much had changed about her otherwise.

The narration in the first paragraph is basic, reflective. It works like a rubber-band propeller, gently twisting for the release to come in the paragraph that follows it—the grandmother like a ghost ship, having recently lost her son, Karl Ove's father. The third is, in terms of syntax and image, very simply written, but it brings a surprisingly strong emotional clench. These paragraphs come after a long, remarkable section, one of the great triumphs of Book One, in which vodka brings the grandmother back from seeming dementia, almost in the manner of L-dopa in Oliver Sacks's *Awakenings*, and sets her to telling stories, giving Karl Ove and his brother an evening of her true company again. The next day, only a trace of that familiar self remains—this whistling and drumming. His grandmother's habit soothes Karl Ove, he's happy to grasp onto it, but it also sets a baseline, marking the gulf between the relative light-heartedness of then and the confusion and near-oblivion of now. Alcohol refueled her briefly, but now she is switched off again and drifting away, with only a drumbeat left unchanged from the past.

In her essay "Two Directions for the Novel," Zadie Smith describes her frustration with lyrical realism. "Everything must be made literary," she writes of Joseph O'Neill's "perfectly done" novel *Netherland*. "Nothing escapes. […] Even the mini traumas of a middle-class life are given the high lyrical treatment." As if in reaction, Knausgaard's style avoids phrase-making. It insists that nothing should be lost to a writer's anxious attempts to say whatever's said just so. This is not anti-literary—just as a tea lover isn't bound to choose doilies and tea cozies.

As I've said, one of Knausgaard's themes is our tendency to subordinate and tame the world beyond ourselves, reducing it to metaphor, which is to say humanizing it, and taking that imposed new skin to be its essence. Karl Ove describes this with an edge of sarcasm: "The limits of that which cannot speak to us—the unfathomable—no longer exist. We understand everything, and we do so because we have turned everything into ourselves." Perhaps surprisingly, given what some have said about the egotism of the project, Knausgaard resists doing this. He doesn't claim to understand everything, doesn't curl everything into the dimensions of his own knowledge. He opts against drawing out implication, just as Deresiewicz argues in *The Nation*. "Understanding the world," Karl Ove narrates skeptically, "requires you to take a certain distance from it."

And distance prevents the engagement that brings meaning. "Meaning requires content, content requires time, time requires resistance. Knowledge," on the other hand, "is distance, knowledge is stasis and the enemy of meaning." *My Struggle* hopes—it's almost a form of prayer—that attentiveness might be enough.

Δ

The confusion about genre in *My Struggle* comes up for reasons both obvious and not so obvious. It comes up because the main character's name is Karl Ove Knausgaard. It comes up because this Karl Ove, like Knausgaard, studied in Bergen and grew up on the island of Tromøya and then in the town of Kristiansand. He wrote a debut novel called *Out of the World* and an angel-obsessed second novel called *A Time for Everything*. But maybe most confusing is the diary element in *My Struggle*. Karl Ove at times narrates what's happening as he writes books that we recognize as Knausgaard's own.

A world in which novels can be published as nonfiction allows for a beautiful slippage, such as the one that had people reading Daniel Defoe's *Memoirs of a Cavalier* as the memoirs of an actual cavalier for more than 40 years after the author's death. It's tempting to let *My Struggle* pass, likewise, as nonfiction. What are J. M. Coetzee's *Boyhood* and *Youth*? What is Thomas Bernhard's *Wittgenstein's Nephew*? But I care too deeply about the novel's ability to reinvent itself, and we can only decide it has happened again here if we agree that *My Struggle*—never mind the layers of fact it contains—is not a memoir.

In cases like W. G. Sebald's *The Rings of Saturn* and other books that lie on the cusp between fiction and fact, the conversation is often about dispute and indeterminacy. With Knausgaard, though, there has been a naive acceptance, a sweet ingenuousness about the nature of the project. Hari Kunzru describes this phenomenon in *The Guardian*, but then seems to join in: "Many critics treat *My Struggle* straightforwardly as memoir, praising it as some kind of unusually neutral transposition from life into art. In Norway it was published as a novel, a small provocation that the English-language publishers have dispensed with." James Wood, whose 2012 essay in *The New Yorker* introduced Book One to the English-speaking world, writes: "*My Struggle* is not really a novel but the first book of a six-volume autobiography." His essay is called "Total Recall." Lerner, in *London Review of Books*, writes that Knausgaard "appears to just write down everything he can recall (and he appears to recall everything)." The key, as when Kunzru describes the seemingly "painfully banal," is that word *appears*.

Knausgaard says he considered *My Struggle* a novel all through writing it. His Norwegian publisher, he told me, wanted to call it a memoir, but he felt that his approach—what he wanted to do and to convey—could only be sustained in a novel. At McNally Jackson he spoke similarly:

I did *exactly* the same thing as in my two other novels. […] It's not about representing myself, it's not about telling about my life, but it's more like a search into it like a novel will search into something. And it's looking for something other than my own life, something *in* my life. And in doing that I used all the tools of a novel.

What was it, then, that Knausgaard couldn't stomach when he grew "tired of fiction"? In the *Bookforum* interview, he classifies TV-news stories and newspaper articles with films and books as fiction; the distinction for him is not whether something happened, but how the account is packaged or structured. In Book Two, Karl Ove has the same concern: "It was a crisis, I felt it in every fiber of my body. […] [A]ll this fiction, whether true or not […] saw the same." He was bucking against not the novel as such but a certain kind of story-formation, a particular structural expectation, a "continuous dramatization of the world" (*Bookforum*). This distaste for pre-commodified shapes freed him to create what Ben Lerner has called an "immersive environment." "What is a work of art," Karl Ove goes on, "if not the gaze of another person?"

So in what way is *My Struggle* fictional? The answer comes in the form of a paradox. Karl Ove tells us his memory of childhood is worse than spotty:

Apart from one or two isolated events that Yngve and I had talked about so often they had almost assumed biblical proportions, I remembered hardly anything from my childhood. That is, I remembered hardly any of the events in it. But I did remember the rooms where they took place. I could remember all the places I had been, all the rooms I had been in. Just not what happened there.

And yet events from his childhood are reproduced with a rare degree of detail. In other words, the fidelity here is not to the particulars of a life as they happened, but to something else.

Whether Karl Ove's memory resembles Knausgaard's, having Karl Ove *say* he forgets his childhood serves a powerful technical purpose. It is MSG for our imaginations, amping up the feeling of lifelikeness by making every detail seem not remembered but lived—not the resurrection of a (forgotten) past but the attentive inhabiting of a (bygone) present. It puts us back there, in a time the adult Karl Ove doesn't remember.

Through it all, we get the same piercing specificity. Karl Ove wavers between what he thinks he remembers (in Book Two, "I held grudges, and every single one of these incidents over the last year lay somehow stored inside me") and what he thinks he *doesn't* remember ("From my own childhood I remember only a handful of incidents"). Yet never do we read even a slight hesitation like *her shirt might have been blue.* Instead it's: "The clock on the department store wall said ten minutes to three. Perhaps it would be best to have a haircut now to avoid having to rush it at the end." Life is now. We are with Karl Ove in the moment, and our understanding that this present is also the past gives the added jolt that *now* feels eternal. Nothing is lost.

All the while, memory loss runs alongside as a theme. In Book Two, Karl Ove meets his best friend, Geir, at college in Bergen (Francine Prose, in *Harper's*, mistakenly treats the Geir from his childhood as the same person), but they don't grow close until Karl Ove leaves his first marriage and arrives in Sweden, where, after 12 years apart, he stays with Geir. "The only scene I remember with him," Karl Ove tells us, thinking back on college, "was in the bar at Fekterloftet in Bergen. Him laughing and saying: You're an existentialist!" In this section—Karl Ove's first days in Sweden—the action is almost exclusively taken up by their long conversations, two men just getting reacquainted. Their different ways of thinking, depicted in long bouts of dialogue—the turns in Geir's rhetoric, the contours of the back-and-forth—form a landscape as particular as the buildings and streets of Stockholm, but evanescent. Geir seems to be a better repository of Karl Ove's past than Karl Ove himself (and here we see another sly instance of the paradox):

"I don't remember a thing from then. And I've burnt all the diaries and manuscripts I wrote in those days."

"Burnt?" Geir questioned. "Not thrown away but burnt?"

I nodded.

"Dramatic," he said. "But then you were like that when you were in Bergen, too."

"Was I?"

"Oh yes."

"But you weren't?"

"Me? No. No, I wasn't."

This is not the sparring of two friends remembering the past differently. It's openhanded questioning by a man who, waiting for Geir in the train station just minutes before, wasn't sure he'd remember what his long-ago acquaintance looked like. That it appears in what for Knausgaard would be a meticulously remembered years-old conversation is a wonderfully comic provocation—it brought me to laughter as I read. Geir says to Karl Ove later, "There's no safer place for secrets than in you. […] You forget everything. Your brain's like Swiss cheese without the cheese."

At one point while Karl Ove is in Kristiansand cleaning his grandmother's house, he takes a walk through town. "Above me," he tells us,

the entire sky had opened. What a few hours earlier had been plain, dense cloud cover now took on landscapelike formations, a chasm with long flat stretches, steep walls, and sudden pinnacles, in some places white and substantial like snow, in others gray and as hard as rock […].

A black Golf was parked by the bus stop beside the newsstand, and the driver, a young man in shorts, clambered out, wallet in hand and darted into the shop, leaving the car idling.

Such details as these would not be remembered 10, 20, in some cases more than 30 years later. Agreeing, a memoirist friend said that Knausgaard meant only to evoke a kind of thing, as if to say, "It was like that, this is how it felt." But the more I've read and reread Knausgaard with my friend's corrective in mind, the more I'm convinced that *My Struggle*, even in the sections that most read like memoir, such as for example the greater part of Book Two, is a very different case. Not just the clothes and passersby, but the actions taken and words said—the conversations about particular books, described as happening years ago—are mostly minute details of the kind one might forget the next week. That is, if all of the details ranging from who was in the room, what was discussed, what food was cooked, and what people wore represent just "the kind of thing that happened," then none of it happened as it's written. Knausgaard has constructed a deeply convincing simulacrum of days, which can fool us into thinking he lived those days and in that order.

The semblance of completeness gives readers a myth to embrace: we can fantasize that, if Knausgaard remembers his entire life exactly as it happened, we can recover ours too. Maybe we'll denature old sadnesses and humiliations by controlling them, discovering the minor events that caused such big feelings to linger. Maybe we'll have the power to re-own, reoccupy, relive the good moments—even the small good moments in otherwise bleak days. Knausgaard's method suggests that the past might still exist.

Δ

How do we choose the songs we seem to hum at random? Why, around a campfire, do we tell this story instead of that one? The husband in Anne Tyler's novel *Breathing Lessons* is constantly giving himself away by whistling. As I remember it, he doesn't talk much, but his wife can figure out what he's thinking by recalling the lyrics of the tune on his lips. By the same sure instinct, or quiet design, Knausgaard too is always telling to a purpose. His attentiveness is not simple.

At the start of Book Two, a man sitting in the kitchen at a child's birthday party reminds Karl Ove of a man at an earlier party, shortly before Vanja, his first child, was born. The subject up to this point is parenthood, the rewards and humiliations of being a deeply involved father. As soon as we meet him, we leave the mysterious man at the kitchen table. Was he there at all? The jump to Micke the boxer at the earlier party feels associative. Two men, two parties, the happenstance of a similar build, and suddenly in a flashback an incident is being narrated. Linda, Karl Ove's wife, gets stuck in a bathroom—even the locksmith called in to free her can't do the job; he says the door needs to be kicked in. But the bookish Karl Ove can't bring himself to try. He is reduced to asking Micke, who comes over, readily splits open the door to free her, and returns to his conversation by the window. The helplessness and inconsequentiality Karl Ove feels suddenly extend the theme of smallness-in-the-landscape beyond parenting and recall the humiliations of Book One.

After a brief return to the birthday party (the mysterious man makes Karl Ove see himself "as the weak, trammeled man I was"), Karl Ove's ruminations take us to his oldest daughter's daycare, referred to in Don Bartlett's translation, which tends to use British forms, as a "nursery." Again it's easy to feel in the flow of the prose that these leaps are motivated by Karl Ove's irrepressible urge to tell. Vanja doesn't go to the nursery anymore. Now her younger sister, Heidi, does. But the point isn't the nursery itself: as with Micke the boxer, a particular incident is being called up and told at this moment because of its resonances and implications. Meaning builds from juxtaposition. *This* placed alongside *that*. At a meeting of the parents' cooperative that runs Vanja's school, again the theme is smallness. Karl Ove suffers along with his wife: "I had no idea what to think about the matter under discussion, and it was Linda who, with a faint blush, weighed the pros and cons on behalf of the family, with the whole assembly staring at her."

Back at the birthday party the girls are playing, and what happens between them, with no express note of the connection, is about assertion of self or its failure, the navigating of relative strength. Vanja has learned to copy rituals or reactions she doesn't understand, and her friend Stella makes fun of her for it, calling her a parrot. A description of this friend takes us back to the nursery, where in another flashback we see Karl Ove negotiating power dynamics with Stella, who kicks his calves again and again. This leads to a further digression; like Jacob's ladder they *seem* to spill forward, but in this second volume the theme of power relations, negotiating power, attempting to preserve stature and self-respect while not threatening that of others, remains a constant—how to balance self and otherness, the inner and the outer, the personal urge and the social demand. Karl Ove has a facility for the required cooperative nursery duty: "I had worked a lot in institutions before." And two of the boys in Vanja's cohort love his company. "A third boy, on the other hand, the oldest one there, immediately discovered one of my weak spots by taking a bunch of keys from my pocket while we were at the table eating." We're once again in the territory of Micke the boxer. It's bad enough that the boy asks if Karl Ove is an adult. But then a member of the staff and finally his daughter step in to help him, just as Micke did. He doesn't ask for help this time, but they see he needs it. And he wonders how. "Drank some water, feeling my face strangely flushed over such a tiny matter. Was that what Olaf, the head of the nursery, saw?"

In the midst of a flow as natural and irregular as a brook's, Knausgaard returns us to the birthday party with such a visceral understanding of fault lines and tensions that they don't have to explicitly reappear for us to feel their influence. Karl Ove retreats to the bathroom: "Met my eyes in the mirror, so dark and in a face so rigid with frustration I almost started with alarm at the sight." The tumbles from scene to scene masquerade as associative. They are casual, often conversational; they are a trope. And behind them: the suspended breath that puts a party on hold to return to it richer, complicated by the ever-deepening history of the tangled relationship between Karl Ove and Linda, the two who form the center of this volume.

If we think of *My Struggle* as a transcript from life, we miss some of its playfulness and some of its pleasures. In the middle of Book Two, Karl Ove narrates what happened on an evening many years back. He and Linda are hosting a dinner party, and after their guests leave, Karl Ove sits at a computer and flies, by means of Google Earth, to Argentina—the first substantial mention of that country in a novel whose working title was "Argentina." He spies on a small town, Rio Gallegos, then moves up the coastline of what he suspects is Patagonia to Puerto Deseado, until we're touring the port and river in Buenos Aires, finally reaching its city center and looking for the essence of literature there, the namesake theater of the great progenitor of the modern Western novel: "I zoomed in on where Teatro Cervantes ought to be, but the image resolution was too poor, everything blurred into contourless green and gray, so I turned off the computer."

This artful arrival brings him to Cervantes, the progenitor of all epics of the everyday. *Don Quixote* is an ancestor to *My Struggle*—another multi-book novel that sets a quest or struggle in the ordinary. Don Quixote jousts against windmills thinking them knights, as if he could restore the concept of honor; Karl Ove, thinking them exemplars of something beyond ourselves, tilts at diapers and cleaning supplies and meals around the table as if he could rediscover the conditions of the sublime. He looks to Cervantes, but the precedent offers no guidance, the quest is too personal: "I zoomed in [...] everything blurred [...] I turned off the computer."

At Community Bookstore, I asked the last question. This was before Knausgaard and I had met. "You've said you don't have a good memory for your childhood." "No—I don't," he said, shaking his head. I'd addressed him as if he were the character Karl Ove, not knowing whether the man himself had said any such thing. But there he'd gone and confirmed it. "And yet the childhood in the book is written with such detail. How did you think about memory while you were writing this book?" In response, Knausgaard described entering a trance state as he wrote. He said, "I knew things were going well when the next morning I read what I'd written the day before and didn't recognize it as my own."

It was a fascinating confession. Rereading didn't put him back in old remembered days. It gave him a shock of discovery. In the *Hazlitt* interview he seems to extend the thought: "For me it's obvious that this isn't about remembering things, this is about staging or re-staging something that I have inside of me." It may just be that the question of adherence to fact is altogether beside the point.

PART III: EVERYTHING IS SIGNIFICANT

> all of it perforce ordinary because it […]
> happens, in different forms, to everyone.
> —James Wood, "Total Recall"

In *My Struggle*, Knausgaard pays profound attention to *things*. He takes the side "of trying, and *failing*, to speak about the thing itself" (to quote the novelist Tom McCarthy about his own, very different project) "and not just ideas about the thing. Of saying 'Jug. Bridge. Cigarette. Oyster. Fruitbat. Windowsill. *Sponge*.'" Readers of Book One will smile at the correspondences here. Cigarette. Windowsill. Sponge. The sublime that Knausgaard tilts at is reluctantly material: the physical world is what we have, yet we know it's more than we can understand. If we look closely enough, long enough, and honestly enough, and resist imposing enchantments, we might yet find what otherwise remains invisible.

The difficulty is noticing, freeing repetition from automatism. In Book Three, the neighbors in Karl Ove's housing "estate" light bonfires to clear leaves and other detritus from their gardens in spring: "Another world was revealed with the fire, and departed with it again. This was the world of air and water, earth and rock, sun and stars, the world of clouds and sky, all the old things that were always there and always had been, and which, for that reason, you didn't think about."

41

Coming only once a year, these fires break through the skin of metaphor that we impose on the physical world, and assert themselves as alien to human meanings. To produce this same effect in us, the narrative uses focus: everyday rituals that in most books are left out are here atomized and repeated—the things of our lives most familiar to us, yet most overlooked, ignored, habituated, are brought into balance with the rest, restored to the place they hold in our days, which in the context of a novel gives them hyperreal presence. When Karl Ove goes, as he often does, from his writing apartment to the bench across the street, we see his movements broken down step-by-step: he scoops the coffee, pours water over it, walks out, sits on the bench, and, as he smokes, watches passersby and notices the conditions of sky and snow. Cigarette. Teakettle. Spoon. Cup. Water. Clothes. Bench. Street. Like a curve chopped into enough segments that each piece looks straight, these objects float free from their uses. They appear nearly still-framed, the focus transferred from action to object, from purpose to materiality, from change to condition.

But the point, as the novel plays it out, isn't pure thinginess. The point is the essential humanness of our tie to the physical. As so often in this profoundly literary work, the theme finds expression in a passage about reading. Karl Ove celebrates Tolstoy's habit of narrating sequences of action for their own sake, seemingly inessential to the story he's telling. "There are long descriptions of landscapes and space, customs and costumes," as Karl Ove describes it, "a rifle barrel smoking after a shot has been fired, the report reverberating with a faint echo, a wounded animal rearing up before falling down dead, and the blood steaming as it flows to the ground."

Then he turns to Dostoevsky, and the difference between the two echoes the earlier shift from the Romantics' rearing landscapes to the emotion-drenched backdrops of Edvard Munch:

> This preponderance of deeds and events for their own sake does not exist in Dostoevsky, there is always something lying hidden behind them, a drama of the soul, and this means there is always an aspect of humanness he doesn't include, the one that binds us to the world outside us.

Books for Karl Ove are both things and portals, miniature big bangs that expand into space-times of their own. Before they gain a deeper significance in his life, books are matter-of-fact objects, sometimes to be hidden from his father like candy. They let him escape when he can't leave the house, but rarely do we hear about what's inside them; the young Karl Ove's deeper fascination is with the records he borrows from his older brother. In Book Two we see a shift, initiated by uncle Kjartan, a poet. Kjartan's immersion in the world of books seems almost neurotic, a severe dissociation from the things of the everyday world. For Kjartan it's as if the actual and intellectual don't co-exist, which Karl Ove notices in a brilliant, funny passage:

[I]t didn't matter that it was Christmas Eve, that the mutton ribs, potatoes, mashed rutabaga, Christmas ale and aquavit were on the table; [Kjartan] talked about Heidegger, from within, without a single communicative link to the outside world, it was *Dasein* and *Das Man*, it was Trakl and Hölderlin, the great poet Hölderlin, it was Heraclitus and Socrates, Nietzsche and Plato, it was the birds in the trees and the waves in the fjord, it was man's *Dasein* and the advent of existence, it was the sun in the sky and the rain in the air, the cat's eyes and the plummeting waterfall. With his hair sticking out in all directions, his suit askew and his tie full of stains he sat there talking, his eyes aglow, they were really glowing, and I will always remember it, for it was pitch-dark outside, the rain was beating against the windows, it was Christmas Eve in Norway 1986, our Christmas Eve, the presents were under the tree, everyone was dressed up, and the sole topic of conversation was Heidegger. Grandma was shivering, Grandad gnawing at a bone, Mom listening attentively, Yngve had stopped listening. As for me, I was indifferent to everything, and above all happy it was Christmas. But even though I didn't understand a word of what Kjartan said, and nothing of what he wrote, nor anything of the poems he praised with such passion, I did understand intuitively that he was right [...].

The entire novel, seen in a certain way, is a record of that struggle between abstract idea-making and immersion in the real; it is the whole of which this passage is a holographic shard: *My Struggle* is a book, therefore bookish, yet its content is the mutton and stained tie as much as—really much more than—Heidegger and Hölderlin, the grandly literary "cat's eyes and the plummeting waterfall."

Δ

With length and the narrative equivalent of patience, with a discovery of grandeur in the common surroundings and a structural insistence that everything is significant, Knausgaard infuses the ordinary with the epic. He does this also by giving each moment consequence in a fated forward spill, while, against the broader sweep, not remaining anywhere for long. (This seems strange to say about a book capable of holding for dozens of pages on a birthday party, but Deresiewicz notes it too.) *My Struggle* gives us the sense not that the lives in the novel are extraordinary, but that all of us partake of the epic, that ordinary life is where we should hunt for grails, that we should not give up on majesty simply because we're without dragons and kings—and angels. The epic lies in and around us, just as the physical world, ourselves included, is what's left of the divine.

Don Quixote marks the great turning point in Western literature from the medieval to the modern, from the romance to the novel. The Man of La Mancha, having missed the memo, carries with him into the world the assumption of the heroic—but what he finds is everywhere resolutely the everyday, whatever he may make of it. As pun, artifact, philosophy, *Don Quixote* is a fulcrum between the extraordinary and the ordinary. It slings literature over the back of a nag and hauls it, comically resisting, toward the domestic and unremarkable. And yet ... Don Quixote insists on the heroism of the everyday, using terms that he's inherited and will not abandon. The neighboring farm girl is his lady Dulcinea, and any objection will be dismissed as piffle. The ignored is made central; the small, by means of attention, scope, and scale, is rendered epic.

Δ

In the series of lectures that became *Aspects of the Novel* (1927), E. M. Forster wrote as close to a set of rules for the novel as an art form can tolerate. He distinguishes between story and plot, describes some conventions of literary character-making—and then pauses to acknowledge that his loose "apparatus suited for Fielding or Arnold Bennett" isn't enough to compass the likes of James Joyce, Herman Melville, Virginia Woolf, and Laurence Sterne. He classes these exception-writers as either "fantastical" or "prophetic."

At first glance, Knausgaard doesn't seem to fit into either of these categories. After all, Deresiewicz fears he'll be "enthroned" as the "apotheosis of realism." But then it starts to come clear: what could be more unlikely than the recovery of every lost detail from our lives? Forster writes: "The other novelists say 'Here is something that might occur in your lives,' the fantasist says 'Here's something that could not occur.'" Into this category Forster puts Virginia Woolf—even specifically *To the Lighthouse*, which, in the story it tells, feels resolutely true-to-life. He describes the category this way, writing about Woolf and Sterne:

> They start with a little object, take a flutter from it, and settle on it again. They combine a humorous appreciation of the muddle of life with a keen sense of its beauty. There is even the same tone in their voices—a rather deliberate bewilderment, an announcement to all and sundry that they do not know where they are going.

"Novels of this type," he adds,

> have an improvised air, which is the secret of their force and charm. [...] It is truer of them than of most books that we can only know what is in them by reading them, and their appeal is specially personal. [...] I would rather hedge as much as possible, and say that they ask us to accept either the supernatural or its absence.

Even this hedging seems to prefigure Knausgaard, whose novel insists that the supernatural is absent, then aims at the super natural. Knausgaard told *Bookforum*: "I want to evoke all the things that are a part of our lives, but not of our stories—the washing up, the changing of diapers, the in-between-things—and make them glow."

Then there's the uncanny coincidence that the fabulism Forster mentions first, the hard-to-accept presence that can sometimes enter novels of this kind, is angels—as if these passages were written in anticipation of a Norwegian whose second novel is populated with them. Is *My Struggle* so different from the earlier book? As Kunzru puts it, "If a reader comes to [*A Time for Everything*], as I did, after *My Struggle*, its exotic subject matter seems like a skin over a familiar body."

Knausgaard, as reader and writer, is drawn to fabulism, and his intent gaze in *My Struggle* on the world-as-it-is comes not as his only option but as an act of intention and willpower. We can see this clearly in Book Three, where he lets in the kinds of things a child believes but an adult no longer can:

> The shadows that descended over the ground outside were so long and distorted that they no longer bore any resemblance to the forms that created them. As though they had sprung forth in their own right, as though there existed a parallel reality of darkness, with dark-fences, dark-trees, dark-houses, populated by dark-people, somehow stranded here in the light, where they seemed so misshapen and helpless [...]. Oh, isn't that why shadows get longer and longer in the evening?

They are reaching out for the night, this tidal water of darkness that washes over the earth to fulfill for a few hours the shadows' innermost yearnings.

These natural fabulisms of childhood are gradually lost to the adult, who then does best to look intently and unflinchingly, though with a childlike focus, seeing the world afresh. Knausgaard emphasizes this kinship between the novel's attention and a child's by juxtaposing the adult Karl Ove's sequence of attention—

I forked the last bit of potato, yellow against the white plate, and raised it to my mouth. While I was chewing I gathered the remaining pieces of meat on my plate, loaded them onto my fork with the knife, together with some onion rings from the salad, swallowed and lifted the rest to my mouth. The man who had taken the chair was on his way to the counter with the older man, whom I guessed to be his wife's father, since none of his characteristic facial features were recognizable in the older man's more ordinary face.

—with his infant daughter Vanja's: "She pointed to some pigeons pecking at crumbs under a table. Then she looked up and pointed at a seagull sweeping past in the wind." Her focus is a smaller version of his, from the down-and-close to the up-and-farther-off, taking in patterns with a quiet, observant awe.

Knausgaard's jagged mountain of words establishes its own "distance between reality and the portrayal of reality." That is, wanting no distance at all, the novel attempts to substitute itself for reality: Pygmalion's sculpture insisting it's alive. And of course it fails, leaving us the measure of the distance that remains—the very space where we can begin to see the full incomprehensibleness of being. There's a playful moment in Book Two, both defiant and accepting, when life and art face each other like two mirrors passing an image back and forth. Karl Ove plates a third lobster for dinner guests and

> something about the consistency made me think it was artificial, like plastic. The red color, wasn't there something unnatural about that, too? And all the attractive, intricate details, like the grooves in the claws or the armor-like tail shell: didn't they look as if they had been forged in the workshop of a Renaissance craftsman?

Momentarily, life resembles art; reality doesn't seem real. But of course this *isn't* life. It's not a lobster, it's a craftsman's depiction of one. The alien physicality of the thing asserts itself: once it can be seen beyond its usefulness as soon-to-be dinner, the animal shocks with ever-finer detail until it almost seems that someone must have made it. As in fact someone did, this "real" lobster that we find in words. The artificial can feel so entirely present. A quick mention of the Renaissance is enough to recall an earlier mode of art, those paintings that, as Karl

Ove tells us in Book One, "always retained some reference to visible reality."

The everyday turns epic precisely here—when its seldom-tapped capacity to take us beyond our knowledge systems, our "fields," allows the grandeur of materiality to seep in, sublimely alien. Knausgaard generally rejects achieving this through metaphor, because he resists further mystifications. He doesn't want, as so many have, to make the familiar strange, he wants to make it visible, allow us to see it again. Each cornflake. Each cup of coffee. Each shortcut through the woods. The foreignness arises naturally, just as when we repeat a word until it stops making sense and we can hear its sounds as if for the first time.

Δ

But it's not so simple, those cornflakes that Ben Lerner singled out when he reviewed Book Three in the *London Review of Books*.

In his piece, Lerner asks, "If your attention as a writer is so egalitarian that your memoir describes a bowl of cornflakes and, say, your brother's face with the same level of detail, how do we determine a hierarchy of value?" The question is penumbral in *My Struggle*; the book seems to ask it everywhere without putting the question directly. But the narrative also provides possible answers. We feel a spirit weight on places and objects. Those cornflakes, so plainly physical and unresponsive—they're just cornflakes!—also carry the joy of Karl Ove's first day of school and the heaviness of his fear of his father, another powerful emotional transference onto things and actions, as James Wood points out about the housecleaning in Book One. For Karl Ove's sanity, the daily associations need to be, and are, stripped back, leaving the cornflakes so bare that it can seem the only point of the narrative is to gaze at those bumps and ridges, and to compare soggy and crunchy, as if those details had the same import as the shape of his father's hand.

But just moments before, his father has yelled at him for joyously brushing his teeth, and sent him to his room. Will he punish Karl Ove for liking the cornflakes too much? The scene held me in suspense—I expected a sudden lashing-out. But Karl Ove, a compartmentalizer, sets aside his fear in favor of close inspection.

We first learn that Karl Ove's father beats him only years and hundreds of pages after the fact, in dialogue, in Book Two, when the adult Geir (Karl Ove's confidant) reveals it in an aside to their mutual friend Helena, in order to set his own father's behavior in relief: "He never hit me in the face and he never hit me on the spur of the moment, like Karl Ove's father did."

I asked Knausgaard if these avoidances were intentional. In answer he said that as he was writing Book One his touchstone was Peter Handke's book about his mother's suicide, *A Sorrow Beyond Dreams*, in which, as Knausgaard expresses it in an essay, the mother is "not represented, only referred to." This is exactly what I feel reading Book One—that Karl Ove's father is more absent than present. By Book Three, fear is less the subject and the father emerges more fully; still, some of the biggest events happen off-stage—the emotions they stir suppressed by the comfort of presence, the thereness of what's here, the world as it is.

There's often an imbalance, especially in childhood, between the emotions we feel and the events that cause them. This becomes one of Knausgaard's major themes early on. In the first volume, we see young Karl Ove's terror, yet his father never turns violent. He mocks Karl Ove's stutter on occasion, he isn't warm, but the magnitude of the boy's fear suggests something as yet unseen. Karl Ove hides in his upstairs room, spies down to see if his father is coming into the house, and we don't entirely know why. Where is the event? Where is the action? His outsized inner life, his terror, is the acute drama of childhood, and Knausgaard enacts it in scenes that remain paradoxically quiet, teasing our expectations.

Knausgaard's held breath plays powerfully here: what will he reveal and when? I had no idea from page to page how the father would react. It was only gradually—with some of the mistakes he makes as a parent, the maybe unwitting belittlements which as a father I always wish I could take back—that I realized nothing more dire would happen, and felt how skillfully Knausgaard had reproduced that almost inexpressible disconnect between childhood reactions and their causes, which, until now, novelists have succeeded mostly in writing *about* rather than writing, and which I would have called insusceptible to dramatizing.

Milan Kundera touches on this in *The Art of the Novel*, in which he writes that "knowledge is the novel's only morality"—indicating not that novelists should tell all, but that the novel advances when it reveals elements of consciousness so integral to our seeing that ordinarily they themselves can't be seen.

Δ

It's time for me to give the author his name back. Karl Ove. By using his own name for the protagonist and saying he wanted to write everything, by emphasizing that he wrote 20 pages a day and changed nothing, Karl Ove encouraged myth-making. Plenty of other speculations and assumptions have developed on their own. I want to examine two of the most prevalent.

The first is as common as they come: the myth of the overnight success. I had the impression from much that I read (and from photos I'd seen) that Knausgaard was an unliterary man practically thumbing his nose at the book world, an accidental writer who'd achieved greatness by happenstance. Maybe he'd spent the last decade touring Scandinavia on a motorcycle, but certainly not perfecting an art. This impression seems to infect even some who've read the books, and threatens to give us bad Knausgaard knockoffs for years to come. By this logic, to imitate him is simple: you write out your life, the Toll House cookies your mother made and all the different days she made them, what you did on those days and where you went, and the Sara Lee cakes, and the cakes your grandmother made, employing the technique of the flashback. Write the anecdotes as they come to you—a scene for each holiday with your mother's parents, and every time you ate with them at a restaurant, and after that add everything that doesn't involve food, down to the times you paid quarters to feed the ducks, and went to museums, and toured factories (wait, this is my life, not his…). If you're interesting and sexy enough and remember everything that happened to you, readers will stampede in your direction—all that stuff you hear about "craft" is the sheerest claptrap.

For his whole life and longer, Faulkner was misunderstood as unschooled in the tradition, ignorant of what had been done in literature, his books the accidental achievement of a natural. How he talked about his work—which had everything to do with how he situated himself in relation to it, allowing him to do what he did—fed that impression. Possibly some of Karl Ove's talk makes us think that his is a dismissive approach. But, in reality, it's a different kind of deep earnestness. In Norway, the conversation about Knausgaard, a friend told me after visiting there this summer, continues to link the popularity of *My Struggle* to a trend Knausgaard certainly benefited from. Deresiewicz describes it in the first paragraph of his *Nation* review:

In 2009, Norwegian state television broadcast "minute-for-minute" coverage of the seven-hour railway journey from Bergen to Oslo. The program was watched, at some point in its duration, by one-quarter of the Norwegian populace. In 2011, the ante was upped: 134 hours of continuous live coverage of the maritime Coastal Express. Half the country tuned in. Two years later came *National Firewood Night*: four hours of chopping, stacking and drying followed by eight hours of a live fireplace. The word of the year in Norwegian, it was announced that December, was *sakte-TV*, "slow TV."

It's true that—in Norway—Karl Ove inherited an audience prepared for length, atomization, the flattening of amplitude. In truth he was up to something very different from slow TV, but he planted *My Struggle* in the soil of that trend. And a myth arose like a beanstalk: all Karl Ove had to do was make coffee page after page and his success was assured.

Instead of resembling a lay person who suddenly performs open-heart surgery, Karl Ove is more like the surgeon who, having spent his life honing techniques in a standard operating room, does multiple surgeries in the backyard with whatever he can find. He's horrified to think how much better it would have gone in the usual sterile field, with his accustomed instruments. But he's convinced he had no choice. To the rest of us— even the other surgeons in the crowd—the thing has the look of happenstance mastery. The patients are thriving.

Sitting on a folding chair on the brick patio behind Community Bookstore in Brooklyn—exhausted after being escorted through a tight press of fans, talking into the clicks of cell-phone cameras, giving an interview to *The New York Times*, and then signing books for a crowd that included people who'd been turned away from the reading—Karl Ove at 10 p.m. gave an impression more modest than assuming or offhand. He's the kind of tall man who sometimes reduces his height for the sake of the people around him. His zip jacket with epaulettes was rumpled—long and narrow, yet still loose on him. He slouched back, sat forward, gazing in a hopeful and searching way. What he seemed to want most of all was to talk about other books, other writers, soccer, European politics, and the boiling situation in Ukraine.

The second great myth is that we meet Karl Ove the man by reading the books. In the audience at McNally Jackson, some people seemed to want the writer in front of them, the charismatic wizard behind the curtain, not to mar what they imagined Karl Ove Knausgaard to be. He talked about his sadness—they worked during the Q&A to deny it. He talked about his need to escape from people—they questioned whether he was telling the truth. They were suturing him into the persona they needed him to occupy—not a solitary man, or miserable, not convinced of the middling quality of much of his book.

That night Knausgaard said, "It's imperfect, my writing. It's something very personal and very imperfect, and I'm showing myself as this stupid character. And then it's very strange to be praised for the opposite. It's impossible for me to deal with […]."

We Americans don't say those kinds of things in public.

It made some people uncomfortable. But unless I'm mistaken there was also hilarity in the room, and a feeling of "yeah sure." Someone made a comment:

> The things you said a few minutes ago, claiming misery, seem to gainsay some of the most wonderful parts of the conversation you had earlier, about horror and wonder going together. […] It seemed to me that one of the great accomplishments of these books is that they attain a kind of gratefulness for the sublime, a happiness that is also misery. I just wondered if you weren't settling that polarity for the sake of comic hyperbole.

Karl Ove ignored the man's conflation of author and work, saying:

> When I just said it? That could be so, yeah. You know, for a cheap laugh. [*Everyone laughed.*] [*Of course.*] But at the same time, it is true—but it's very difficult to talk about, because if you talk about it, it is like you're posing. "Look, I'm a miserable writer." So what can I say? I truly am, you know?

He'd tried to be honest and not shirk the questions, but now it looked like he was answering for effect. He turned to Zadie Smith, asked her permission for something. She nodded, though it wasn't clear she knew what was coming. "I was praising Zadie's book *On Beauty* to her," he went on, "and she said, 'I hadn't read that book in eight years, but recently had to, and I couldn't find one page that didn't make me want to puke.' And that was *On Beauty*, an absolutely fantastic, amazing book, which is brilliant. There you go."

It's easy to feel we know who he is. Smith helped put him in that bind by accepting the drug that the book holds out to us. "What's notable," she writes in *The New York Review of Books*, "is Karl Ove's ability, rare these days, to be fully present in and mindful of his own existence. Every detail is put down without apparent vanity or decoration, as if the writing and the living are happening simultaneously." A remarkable thing to say about a man who retreated from his family for years to write 3,600 pages at more than a hundred a week. But then, look at the rest of us, we who can't unlock from our screens, who layer our days with podcasts and music and other distractions from what's going on around us.

In "Speaking in Tongues," Smith writes of Cary Grant that he "seemed the product of a collective dream, dreamed up by moviegoers in hard times." In this strange time of our dislocation from the physical surround, we take Karl Ove to represent immersion in the world because that's what *My Struggle* seems to promise.

Ours is an era of Based on a True Story. We drool for that.

Δ

Karl Ove has said he wanted to incorporate everything that lives in him as a source, the wellsprings of any possible art. The only element of the novel that he planned from the outset, as he tells it, was the last sentence of Book Six, which goes something like: "And now I'm happy that I'm no longer an author."

Behind Community Bookstore, over our cans of Dale's after the crowd had gone, one of the small team from Archipelago talked about her love of Antonio Porchia, an Argentine poet. She and Karl Ove talked about another Argentine, César Aira. Then he brought up Polish novelist Witold Gombrowicz, one of his idols and touchstones. Gombrowicz did his best work in Argentina, he told us. The place seemed to draw it out of him. As soon as Gombrowicz left for Paris late in his life, it was over—everything he wrote after that was crap. His prose fell apart completely, for the rest of his life.

One's best—Karl Ove said coolly but emphatically—is often tied to a place that somehow seems to allow it or make it possible.

"Argentina." His working title for *My Struggle*.

When he was asked at McNally Jackson the next evening, "Why 'Argentina'?," he didn't mention any of this. Not a word about Gombrowicz or the idea that had so animated him the night before. He called Argentina "a dream country, a dream continent, a dream republic"—a place he'd longed to visit as a child, and thought he never would. "There's a lot of longing in *My Struggle* and for me Argentina was the place the longing was directed."

A man in the audience said "Argentina" wouldn't have made a good title then, because the novel isn't about longing for exotic climes. It isn't about a desire to leave. It looks for satisfaction in the small, in the familiar—a homebody desire sooner than the bug to travel.

Exactly.

I'm reminded of Svidrigailov in *Crime and Punishment*, whose only aim is to go to America. He talks about it incessantly. He's leaving soon, even if no one believes him. He is on his way. And then one day he gets ready and leaves for America—by shooting himself.

In answering the question about Argentina as he did, Knausgaard gave the audience one truth while hiding a still deeper one. His method is visible in this. *My Struggle* is not a confessional space—it is performative, a space where memory and imagination give rise to something new.

"Argentina"—I believe this is key—was a *working* title. It wasn't a prospective actual title, it was a title for the writing of it. It created, by fiat, a place. "Argentina" was to Knausgaard as Argentina was to Gombrowicz, transforming the novel into its own talisman. How to consistently, day by day, overcome the old limiting desire to please people; how to calm the self-doubt natural to a wildly uncertain method? The right soil, the needed grounding, became internal to the project. Knausgaard could move from Norway to Sweden, he could return from Sweden to Norway, he could go anywhere—and always be in Argentina when he sat at his table. In the high-wire act of writing fast and hard and very very long, the only available safety net was an expedient trick of the mind.

A "literary suicide," he has called *My Struggle*. What more is there to say?

William Pierce's fiction has appeared in *Granta, Ecotone*, and elsewhere. He edits, with Sven Birkerts, the literary and cultural magazine *AGNI*.

ARROWSMITH is named after the late William Arrowsmith, a renowned classics scholar, literary and film critic. General editor of thirty-three volumes of *The Greek Tragedy in New Translations*, he was also a brilliant translator of Eugenio Montale, Cesare Pavese, and others. Arrowsmith, who taught for years in Boston University's University Professors Program, championed not only the classics and the finest in contemporary literature, he was also passionate about the importance of recognizing the translator's role in bringing the original work to life in a new language.

Like the arrowsmith who turns his arrows straight and true,
a wise person makes his character straight and true.

— Buddha

Books by

ARROWSMITH

PRESS